More
30 SECOND
MYSTERIES

spinner books

San Francisco • Maastricht • Sydney

ACKNOWLEDGEMENTS

University Games Europe B.V., Australiëlaan 52,
6199 AA Maastricht Airport, Netherlands.

University Games Australia, 10 Apollo Street, Warriewood, Australia 2102.

Retain this information for future reference.

ISBN 1-57528-881-8

Printed in Mexico

07 08 09 10 11 RRD 9 8 7 6 5 4 3 2 1

CONTENTS

INTRODUCTION

Jeff Pinsker and I co-developed dozens of games together, but none were as challenging or memorable as *30 Second Mysteries*™. What a story! Jeff and I decided to invent the ultimate party game for the witty and the precocious. We wanted the game to be quick, tricky, educational and fun. We came up with the title *30 Second Mysteries*™ – and the notion that if players were clever they could solve the mysteries in 30 seconds, and if we were clever we could write them in 30 seconds.

Jeff and I met one snowy day in London at the John Bull Pub to turn our concept into reality. We sat for nearly nine hours and created the game as we consumed one fine British lager after another. The results of our day in London were collected in the first volume of *30 Second Mysteries*™.

Each 30 second mystery is a fun, interactive form of a good old-fashioned whodunit. This third volume, like its predecessors, will entertain you, your friends and your colleagues for hours. It's sure to exercise your logical and critical thinking muscles, as well as tease your funny bone.

We had a great time putting these mysteries together and hope you have even more fun trying to solve them.

Good Luck!

Bob Moog

RULES

OBJECT
To be the first player or team to solve 7 mysteries or score 7 points.

PLAYING THE GAME

• First things first: grab a pen and paper to keep track of your points.

• The youngest player spins first to determine the type of mystery to be solved (i.e. Who, What, Where or Why) and reads the first Case and Mystery from that category out loud to the group. This player acts solely as a reader and may not play until the mystery is solved. The player to the left of the Reader gets the first clue—and the first stab at solving the mystery.

• *If a player guesses the mystery incorrectly (or doesn't have a guess),* the player to his/her left gets the next clue and may then try to crack the case. Play proceeds in a clockwise fashion.

• *If a player guesses the mystery correctly,* s/he earns a point and the player to the Reader's left becomes the new Reader for the next case in the same category. Do not spin again until each player has read a mystery to the group.

• Once all players have acted as the Reader, it is time to spin again! The player to the left of the last person to spin now spins to determine the type of mystery to be solved. S/he is the first Reader for this round.

• *Tip:* Don't forget to jot down the number of the last mystery solved in case you spin the same category more than once, which is likely to happen.

SCORING

First player to guess the mystery scores 1 point. If a player solves the mystery without hearing any clues, s/he earns 2 points.

WINNING THE GAME

The first player to score 7 points wins!

PLAYING ON YOUR OWN

Spin and read the Case and Mystery topic question from the appropriate category. Try to solve the Case using as few clues as possible.

SCORING:

6 points = 1 clue revealed
5 points = 2 clues revealed
4 points = 3 clues revealed
3 points = 4 clues revealed
2 points = 5 clues revealed
1 point = 6 clues revealed
0 points = Incorrect guess!

Read 10 mysteries. Collect 30 points or more and you're a winner!

Case 1

THE CASE

An alcoholic recluse who lives far from the limelight goes into his workplace. He refuses to work in what could be considered "normal" ways, instead preferring to kneel on the floor while he labors. Because of his unique approach, he gains national and then international acclaim, but sabotages his health and dies tragically in the end.

THE MYSTERY

Who was this man and why was he famous?

THE CLUES

The man was American.

A car crash took his life.

The man smoked and drank to excess.

A biopic of his life was released starring Ed Harris.

The man was nicknamed "Jack the Dripper."

CASE 1 SOLUTION

The man is Jackson Pollock, famous for his large-scale Abstract Expressionist artwork composed of dripped, spilled and flung paint.

More 30 SECOND MYSTERIES

WHO

Case 2

THE CASE

A patriot travels on a small horse to a faraway village. Upon arriving, he places part of a nearby bird into his clothing. He then appears quite confused by pronouncing to all within earshot that he has in his possession some Italian pasta.

THE MYSTERY

Who is the patriot and what is the Italian pasta?

THE CLUES

He is visiting a city on the East Coast.

Most people learn about him even before they enter school.

He was popular during the forming of our nation.

His name identifies him as a Northerner.

His story is continually repeated in song.

CASE 2 SOLUTION

The patriot is Yankee Doodle Dandy and the pasta is macaroni.

THE CASE

A stranger barges into a house where two small children wait alone for their mother to come home. The children are scared, but the stranger doesn't seem to notice. Instead, this individual makes the children play games they don't want to play. Eventually the stranger leaves and, surprisingly, the police are not summoned.

THE MYSTERY

Who is the individual and who made him famous?

THE CLUES

The individual arrives wearing a hat, gloves, a bow tie and a fur coat.

The individual likes to play, even on a cold, cold, wet day.

The individual speaks in rhyme.

The individual brings two Things to the house.

A famous Dr. brought him to life.

CASE 3 SOLUTION

The individual is the Cat in the Hat®. Dr. Seuss (Theodor Geisel) made him famous.

More 30 SECOND
MYSTERIES

WHO

Case 4

THE CASE

A boy kills a bear and later grows up to serve his home state in the national leg-islature. He returns to his Southern home, only to be summoned to travel to a desolate place to fight against foreigners. He dies there, but is honored as a hero and is best remembered for his distinctive hat.

THE MYSTERY

Who was the man and from what state did he hail?

THE CLUES

The man was from the "Volunteer State."

The man and his family lived in a log cabin.

Walt Disney made a movie about the man.

The man died at the Alamo in 1836.

The man wore a coonskin cap and was "King of the Wild Frontier."

CASE 4 SOLUTION

The man is Davy Crockett and he was from Tennessee.

Case 5

THE CASE

A government worker is assigned to assist in making the world a better place. The man was born before 1950, but was under 35 years old when he came out of retirement in the 1990s. The man has a strong preoccupation with his attractiveness, but isn't actually attractive. He speaks with an accent, but knows English quite well.

THE MYSTERY

Who is the man and what does he do for a living?

THE CLUES

The man always gets the job done, but isn't very serious about his work.

The man is famous for his dalliances.

The man always has a cast of characters that support him.

The man has bad teeth and a dated fashion sense.

The man is groovy, baby.

CASE 5 SOLUTION

The man is Austin Powers. He's a spy for the British government.

THE CASE

A man walks into a room and people immediately start screaming at him. The man begs the mob not to be mean and tries to calm them by discussing his footwear. The mob continues to scream. He leaves after a few hours, but the crowd disperses only after being reassured that he has gone for good.

THE MYSTERY

Who is the man and why has the mob gathered?

THE CLUES

The man has never been in jail.

The man is used to being yelled at.

The man has a soothing voice and a commanding presence.

The man is famous for his moves, among other things.

The man is a king but does not wear a crown.

CASE 6 SOLUTION

The man is Elvis Presley and the mob has gathered to see him perform.

More 30 SECOND
MYSTERIES
WHO

Case 7

THE CASE

After taking a bad fall, a lost and bewildered young girl suspects she may have been drugged. The girl stumbles upon wild rabbits and a mischievous cat while trying to find her way. She meets many other animated characters and narrowly escapes with her life.

THE MYSTERY

Who is the girl and where has she found herself?

THE CLUES

The girl's ordeal began after a nap on the lawn.

Though she is lost and confused, she goes to a party.

She is encouraged to drink a strange brew, which has a disturbing effect on her.

The girl is quite a character.

Lewis Carroll is responsible for the girl's many adventures.

✪ 21 ✪

CASE 7 SOLUTION

She is Alice and she has found herself in Wonderland.

More 30 SECOND
MYSTERIES

WHO

—·—·—·—·—·—

Case 8

THE CASE

A man in handcuffs stands on a bridge surrounded by a large crowd of people.
Suddenly, the man leaps off the bridge into the cold, fast-moving river below.
Oddly enough, he does not drown, but climbs out of the river safe and sound
and is met by an applauding crowd.

THE MYSTERY

Who was this man and why did he leap into the river wearing handcuffs?

THE CLUES

The people watching knew that the man was going to jump into the river.
Some people were surprised that the man escaped; others expected it.
The man had done similar things before.
The man was a professional magician.
The man died in 1926.

CASE 8 SOLUTION

The man was Harry Houdini, who leapt into the river as part of his performance.

THE CASE

An older lady is kept in dark seclusion for days as a time. When she is allowed out, it is almost always in the morning. She is never fed. Although she is famous and loved by many, no one objects to her treatment.

THE MYSTERY

Who is the older lady and why does no one object?

THE CLUES

The lady is famous for her sweetness.

The lady always wears a collared dress and apron.

The lady is in her forties.

The lady's favorite meal is breakfast.

The lady is made of glass and her apron is a label.

CASE 9 SOLUTION

No one objects because the lady is a bottle of Mrs. Butterworth's™ syrup.

More 30 SECOND
MYSTERIES

WHO

Case 10

THE CASE

A father tenderly cares for his child after its mother has left the two of them. For many months, he protects the child from a dangerous environment, sacrificing his well-being in the process. Eventually, the mother returns and the father immediately goes off to sea, leaving his child behind.

THE MYSTERY

Who is the father and where does he live?

THE CLUES

While the father does go off to sea, he's no sailor.

Without the father, the child would die almost instantly.

The father lives with many other fathers, all in a similar situation.

The mother left for many months but the father expected her return.

The father wears only a tuxedo, but is not human.

CASE 10 SOLUTION

The father is an emperor penguin, living in Antarctica.

Case 11

THE CASE

A man enters a room where a bald man begins talking to him and asking personal questions. The man with no hair then introduces a room full of beautiful models. One by one, the women leave. As each leaves, the bald man offers money for the man to leave, as well. After one hour, the man leaves with $1 million.

THE MYSTERY

Who is the bald man and why did the man leave with $1 million?

THE CLUES

26 models enter the room silently.

The bald man is in his 40s and has shaved his head.

The entire event is filmed and televised by NBC and hosted by the bald man.

To receive the $1 million, the man has to be lucky with numbers.

The event took place after January 2006.

CASE 11 SOLUTION

The bald man is Howie Mandel. The man won $1 million on Deal or No Deal®.

THE CASE

In a packed theatre, an assistant leads a physically challenged man to a seat in the middle of a stage. The man begins to move his head in an odd, irregular fashion as he performs. Instead of being put off by his behavior, the audience is in awe of what he can do and starts to applaud.

THE MYSTERY

Who is the man and what's he doing on the stage?

THE CLUES

A piano is part of his performance.

The man has been performing for 40 years.

He often wears sunglasses.

Motown gave him his start.

When he was young, "Little" preceded his name.

CASE 12 SOLUTION

The man is Stevie Wonder; he's singing and playing the piano.

Case 13

THE CASE

Two young European children ventured into the woods with nothing more than a piece of bread. One day later, they emerged with stories of attempted murder, stolen property and child abuse.

THE MYSTERY

Who were the children?

THE CLUES

The event took place several hundred years ago.

The children were siblings.

They met a woman who invited them to dinner.

The children were not very experienced in orienteering.

The children discovered an edible house during their adventure.

CASE 13 SOLUTION

The children are Hansel and Gretel.

More 30 SECOND
MYSTERIES
WHO

Case 14

THE CASE

A young woman believes that she has heard the divine word and commences to rally her community against its chosen leaders. She becomes a symbol of freedom and conviction, but meets a violent end before her mission is fully realized. Despite her inauspicious demise, she remains a holy hero to many and is remembered for centuries.

THE MYSTERY

Who was the woman and where was she from?

THE CLUES

The woman started to gain fame while in her teens.

The woman lived in the 15th century.

The woman was not a fan of the English.

The woman is best known by her first name.

The woman was declared a saint in 1920.

CASE 14 SOLUTION

Joan of Arc lived in France.

More 30 SECOND
MYSTERIES
WHO

Case 15

THE CASE

A woman sits in an old cabin without any indoor plumbing or electricity, trying desperately to do some meaningful volunteer work. Working only by candlelight, she searches her mind to develop an inspirational message to encourage a small group of revolutionary insurgents. She successfully communicates her inspirational message and her revolutionaries achieve their independent dreams.

THE MYSTERY

Who was the woman and what was the result of her volunteer work?

THE CLUES

The woman was a seamstress.

The revolutionaries spoke English.

The woman's volunteer work led to a new symbol for a new people.

The woman lived in the 18th century.

The woman communicated with blue and red dye on a white background.

CASE 15 SOLUTION

Betsy Ross created the first American flag.

More 30 SECOND
MYSTERIES

WHO

—·—·—·—·—·—

Case 16

THE CASE

In the dark of night, a daring woman performed feats that few in their right mind would consider. Over many years, she put herself and others in harm's way with her hair-raising adventures, but in the end she escaped unscathed. After meeting her, people were never the same again.

THE MYSTERY

Who was this person and what is she famous for?

THE CLUES

People think of the woman as a great American heroine.

What she eventually did for other people, she first did for her family.

In her eyes, all people were equal.

She helped countless people make a safe passage.

The "railroad" was her mode of transportation.

CASE 16 SOLUTION

---

*Harriet Tubman is famous for helping
to free slaves on the Underground Railroad
before the American Civil War.*

More 30 SECOND MYSTERIES

WHO

— · — · —

Case 17

THE CASE

During the light of day, a man trespasses on personal property, taking things that do not belong to him. If no one is home, the man may occasionally go inside and leave hidden messages that can implicate but not indict him.

THE MYSTERY

Who is he and why doesn't he get arrested?

THE CLUES

People anxiously await this man's arrival.

Dogs are not known to be his best friend.

What he takes often travels by air.

He has vowed that weather will not deter his mission.

He wears a blue uniform.

CASE 17 SOLUTION

He's a postman and is delivering/picking up mail.

Case 18

THE CASE

A young woman goes to work in a place with more than 5,000 people. She sweats as she toils and works for less than two hours, but gets paid more than most of the other people in her company make in a month. Even though her effort on this particular day does not result in making any new products, all of the people at her work applaud when she finishes. The next day she goes to another city and does it again.

THE MYSTERY

Who is the young woman and what does she do for a living?

THE CLUES

Some doubt the young woman's skill.

Many people listen to the young woman.

The young woman is very entertaining.

The young woman was born in the 1980s.

Some people think that more than just her initials are B.S.

CASE 18 SOLUTION

The young woman is Britney Spears and she is a pop star.

More 30 SECOND
MYSTERIES

WHO

—-—··—-—··—-—

Case 19

THE CASE

A man travels the world, killing whoever gets in his way. He has mystified officials from Manhattan to Minsk with his lawless escapades, but despite this lifestyle he shows no signs of aging. Even though he seems quite smart, he relies heavily on high-tech tools to get the job done.

THE MYSTERY

Who is he and why isn't he a wanted man?

THE CLUES

Though many have tried, it seems impossible to kill him.

He's fond of high-tech gadgets.

He's unquestionably dapper and likes women.

He's been featured in books and movies.

He likes his martinis shaken, not stirred.

CASE 19 SOLUTION

He's James Bond, a spy employed by the British Secret Service.

More 30 SECOND
MYSTERIES

WHO

_._._._._._._._

Case 20

THE CASE

At the age of 30, a very wealthy man walks out on his life of comfort to begin searching for an elusive treasure. He finds the treasure years later under a tree and spends the rest of his life sharing the treasure with everyone he meets.

THE MYSTERY

Who is this man and what is the treasure that he found?

THE CLUES

The man is the son of a wealthy tribal ruler.

The man lived thousands of years ago.

Though we don't know what he looked like, his likeness can be found all over the world.

By the time he died at about age 80, he was widely regarded as a holy man.

Millions have followed his teachings in the hopes of finding his treasure.

CASE 20 SOLUTION

*The man is Prince Gautama Siddhartha
(or Buddha). The treasure he found was enlightenment.*

More 30 SECOND
MYSTERIES

WHO

Case 21

THE CASE

Out on a boat on a foggy night, some teenagers (along with their pet) accidentally beach on an island that's said to be inhabited by phantoms and ghosts. Nonplussed by the threatening locals, this rogue gang unmasks the villains and continues on their merry way, roaming the country to solve crimes and conundrums of every kind.

THE MYSTERY

Who is the leader of this gang and what's his favorite treat?

THE CLUES

Fear rules this individual's existence.

He's shorter than everyone else in the gang.

He speaks unintelligibly.

Most of his adventures are spooky.

The words "Ruh-roh" occur often in his lingo.

CASE 21 SOLUTION

*Scooby Doo leads the gang and he loves
Scooby Snacks.*

THE CASE

A woman steals into a child's room, intent on taking at least one thing with her when she leaves. The child is not aware of this visitor, but would not be afraid if he knew she was there. Although the woman and child do not know each other, they are vaguely acquainted.

THE MYSTERY

Who is this woman and what does she leave?

THE CLUES

The woman is not doing anything illegal.

The woman is not a witch.

The items the woman takes have no monetary value.

The child is anxious for the woman to come.

The woman's visit proves to be profitable for the child.

CASE 22 SOLUTION

The woman is the Tooth Fairy. She leaves small sums of money.

More 30 SECOND
MYSTERIES

WHO

Case 23

THE CASE

A young man sets sail on an ocean liner, where he meets his one true love. Brief but passionate, their love affair becomes legend, with people around the globe reliving the story over and over again. Sadly, he dies a terrible death in the end.

THE MYSTERY

Who brought this story to the masses and where might one find it?

THE CLUES

Contrary to the fable, he lived on.
A fateful collision makes this story memorable.
The young man claimed to be the king of the world.
It cost $300 million to get this story out.
The story gave some a sinking feeling.

CASE 23 SOLUTION

James Cameron directed the 1997 movie Titanic.
It can be found in video stores everywhere.

THE CASE

An enterprising older man handpicks three buxom young ladies to be his employees. In the line of duty, they'll be expected to use their feminine wiles to achieve their career goals. They are greatly admired, often imitated and years later, brought out of retirement for a comeback.

THE MYSTERY

Who are these women and what were they employed to do?

THE CLUES

They were professionally trained – and coifed.

They live in Los Angeles and are nationally known.

They solve crimes using brains and brawn, but mostly beauty.

Their boss is elusive.

The women are real angels, but they don't have wings.

CASE 24 SOLUTION

They're Charlie's Angels and they worked as undercover detectives solving crimes.

More 30 SECOND
MYSTERIES

WHO

Case 25

THE CASE

A small group of people search each morning for a buried item. Prior to their search, they sit at a table where each has an empty bowl. The item is not of great monetary value, but there will be a dispute over its rightful ownership once it is discovered. The group leader will be forced to step-in and clear up the argument.

THE MYSTERY

Who is the group leader and what are they looking for?

THE CLUES

Only one person at a time can dig for the buried item.

The group will search through wheat, corn, rice and sugar to find the treasure.

The group leader is a woman with great authority.

The group is kin and only the leader is over four-feet tall.

Most likely, a cheap plastic plaything will be uncovered rather than a valuable artifact.

CASE 25 SOLUTION

The group calls the leader "Mom" and they are looking for the prize in a cereal box.

Case 26

THE CASE

A hardened individual from Middle America expresses hatred for his mother. He also expresses anger toward his wife and many other women he's met. His negative attitude doesn't hinder him; instead, it brings him wealth and fame. He is asked to appear on TV and share his message with the country.

THE MYSTERY

Who is this man and what does he do for a living?

THE CLUES

He's known for speaking his mind.

He's very controversial.

Dr. Dre was his mentor.

He hails from an area of Detroit called 8 Mile.

He's appeared at the GRAMMY® Awards.

CASE 26 SOLUTION

He's Eminem (a.k.a. Marshall Mathers) and he's a famous rap star.

More 30 SECOND MYSTERIES

WHO

--- --- --- ---

Case 27

THE CASE

A very young woman comes into great responsibility after the death of her father. Others in her family resent her power and she's forced to flee, as her life may be in jeopardy. She seeks help from neighbors but they mostly just fall in love with her. Finally she dies tragically, though the actual facts of her death are in doubt for years and years to come.

THE MYSTERY

Who is this woman and when did she live?

THE CLUES

She was well educated, especially for a woman of her era.

Intrigue and tragedy were constants in her life.

She was well acquainted with Caesar.

She was the last pharaoh.

Liz Taylor brought her to life in the movies.

CASE 27 SOLUTION

The woman is Cleopatra; she lived in the century
before Christ's birth, around 69 – 30 B.C.

More 30 SECOND
MYSTERIES

WHO

-·-·-·-·-·-·-·-

Case 28

THE CASE

A young woman sustains great physical injuries during an accident. Forced to stay in bed for months on end, she takes up art as a hobby. Though her life is shaped by health problems that persist after the accident, her hobby becomes a great source of joy – and eventually brings her great acclaim.

THE MYSTERY

Who is this woman and who was her husband?

THE CLUES

She is considered an important woman in the history of her line of work.

Many of her pieces were self-portraits.

She hails from Mexico.

She believed in leftist causes and was politically active.

Her husband was a great Mexican muralist.

CASE 28 SOLUTION

She is Frida Kahlo and her husband is Diego Rivera.

More 30 SECOND
MYSTERIES

WHAT

—·—·—·—·—·—

Case 1

THE CASE

A deafening sound cracks through the air on a warm summer's day. People emerge from their homes to see about the racket, only to hear the noise again. Suddenly and without warning, several huge objects come charging into view.

THE MYSTERY

What are these objects and where can they be found?

THE CLUES

The objects are associated with technology.

They aim to dazzle onlookers.

It's not unusual to see the huge objects roll, dive and spin.

They have been an institution of the U.S. Navy since 1946.

The sound barrier is not much of a barrier for these tricksters.

CASE 1 SOLUTION

They are the Blue Angels, airplanes from the U.S. Navy flight team; they travel to air shows around the globe.

THE CASE

Many years ago in the darkness of a blustery and cold mid-western evening, a family decides to make its way to California. Sunshine and beaches await them, but first they have to get there. They plan their route, pack their bags and start the trip to L.A., every minute thankful for the one thing that's making this trip easier and less time consuming.

THE MYSTERY

What helped them make it to California quickly?

THE CLUES

It was once the major East-West artery.

Driving it could be considered an American Odyssey.

Nat King Cole sang about it.

You can get your kicks on it.

Its name includes double digits.

CASE 2 SOLUTION

They are driving the famous Route 66 highway that used to stretch all the way from Chicago to L.A.

Case 3

THE CASE

Chris has just finished 12 hours of work. He knows that he will not earn any money for his day of work; in fact, the place where he works has required him to pay them $10,000 for the past 12 hours. Chris is tired, but excited to return to his place of work tomorrow. On his way home, Chris sees the Empire State Building and the Eiffel Tower.

THE MYSTERY

What is Chris's occupation and where does he live?

THE CLUES

Chris does not work every day.

Chris cannot work alone.

Chris' work requires luck and skill.

Sometimes Chris' work is televised.

Chris works in the state of Nevada.

CASE 3 SOLUTION

Chris is a professional poker player living in Las Vegas.

THE CASE

Each day, Tom goes to work early in the morning. Once at work, he dons a little white outfit and then enters a very cold chamber. Throughout the day, he continues to enter and retreat from the cold chamber, each time returning to his workstation with a heavy package. Tom deals with cows, pigs, chicken and fish, but doesn't live on a farm or near a river.

THE MYSTERY

What is Tom's job and where does he work?

THE CLUES

Tom is obsessive about keeping his work area clean.

Tom hates to create waste.

The animals Tom deals with don't make a sound.

Tom sees his fair share of blood.

Tom's uniform includes an apron.

CASE 4 SOLUTION

Tom is a butcher working in a butcher shop.

Case 5

THE CASE

Each day on the way to work, Kristen and hundreds of other people are controlled by a force that has no arms or legs. While it has no mouth, it can cause Kristen and others to freeze in their tracks. Cars, buses and taxis all fear this incredible heartless enemy, but they also know that it saves their lives every day.

THE MYSTERY

What force has such power over people?

THE CLUES

The effect of the force is immediate, but lasts only a short time.

The force's code involves 3 colored lights.

The force can count, but it only counts backwards.

The force can be seen from a distance.

The force wouldn't be needed if there were no cars.

CASE 5 SOLUTION

A traffic light.

More 30 SECOND
MYSTERIES

WHAT

—— · — · — · — · — · ——

Case 6

THE CASE

Peter Oatman works for the Police Department, but he doesn't carry a gun. In fact, he doesn't even wear a uniform. Nevertheless, Peter is usually on the scene of the crime quickly and he is credited with solving all sorts of crimes.

THE MYSTERY

What is Peter's job?

THE CLUES

Peter is extremely observant.

Peter never arrests anyone.

There are many people with Peter's skills working for the police.

Samples are required to do Peter's job.

Peter works in a lab.

CASE 6 SOLUTION

Peter is a Crime Scene Investigator.

More 30 SECOND
MYSTERIES

WHAT

—·—·—·—·—

Case 7

THE CASE

Sherry enters a business establishment with more than $500 in cash and valuables. After less than 3 minutes, she leaves with none of her valuables, but with a single piece of paper. Sherry isn't upset, doesn't call the police and plans to return to the business establishment again.

THE MYSTERY

What were Sherry's valuables and what type of business did she visit?

THE CLUES

Sherry's valuables include a mink stole and her favorite dress.

Sherry expects to retrieve the 'missing' valuables within a week.

The business routinely exchanges a piece of paper for valuable possessions.

Sherry brought her valuables in not long after she used them.

The business returned the valuables in a better condition than they were delivered.

CASE 7 SOLUTION

Sherry dropped her clothing off at her dry cleaner.

Case 8

THE CASE

Peter is a misunderstood teenager who has a very dangerous night time occupation. He wears a full-body uniform for his graveyard shift and often finds himself falling off of very tall buildings. Often he fights off the attacks of incredibly deranged characters. Peter never gets hurt too badly and appears to win every fight.

THE MYSTERY

What is Peter's last name and what is his night time job?

THE CLUES

Peter lives in New York City with his aunt.

Peter works as a photographer for the local paper.

Peter certainly doesn't have arachnophobia.

Peter's night job has been captured in comics and movies.

Gwen was Peter's girlfriend.

CASE 8 SOLUTION

Peter is Peter Parker and he spends his nights fighting crime as Spider-Man.

Case 9

THE CASE

Bernadette picks up a very sharp object and holds it in her left hand. She then very carefully selects some binding material. Others observe her behavior and nod approvingly. Smiling, like an assassin, Bernadette then grabs a second very sharp object and commences to stab the binding material. After several hours she stops and calmly packs up her things and leaves, taking both sharp objects with her.

THE MYSTERY

What are the sharp objects and what is the binding material?

THE CLUES

Bernadette is in a class.

The binding material comes in many colors.

Bernadette is not a criminal.

Bernadette learned this activity from her mother.

Bernadette is creating clothing.

CASE 9 SOLUTION

Bernadette is in a knitting class. The sharp objects are knitting needles and the binding material is yarn.

More 30 SECOND
MYSTERIES

WHAT

Case 10

THE CASE

Steve hangs out in a bad part of town, and he loves to drink beer. He is often seen gesturing violently with both hands as he talks in a loud voice, even though no one else is nearby. Sometimes he repeats himself three or four times. Although police officers routinely lock up people who drink as much as Steve does and walk around talking to no one, they always leave Steve alone.

THE MYSTERY

What is Steve doing while he gestures with his hands?

THE CLUES

Police officers don't give Steve a second glance; they think he's perfectly normal.

Steve is usually well-dressed.

Steve is not homeless.

Steve likes to use modern technology.

Steve is having a conversation with someone, even though he's alone.

CASE 10 SOLUTION

Steve is wearing a wireless headset; he is talking on his cell phone.

More 30 SECOND
MYSTERIES

WHAT

Case 11

THE CASE

People come from all over the world to view paintings at a well-known location in France. They marvel at the artists' use of color and perspective. Although the paintings are famous, even experts don't know who painted them, or when they were painted.

THE MYSTERY

In what type of "facility" are the paintings housed?

THE CLUES

The paintings have natural subjects.

The paintings are very old.

The paintings are not in a museum.

The paintings were not painted with brushes and paint.

The paintings record everyday events, and celebrate triumphs.

CASE 11 SOLUTION

The paintings are ancient cave paintings.

Case 12

THE CASE

Gavin is wanted by the police for numerous bank robberies, but the police don't know his real name, or what he looks like. Although he's broken into more than a dozen banks and stolen millions of dollars, he has never actually set foot in a bank.

THE MYSTERY

What is the main tool Gavin uses to commit his robberies?

THE CLUES

Gavin does not use weapons.

Gavin always works alone.

It is impossible for bank tellers to identify him, because they have never seen him.

The police don't even bother to review the images captured by the security cameras.

Gavin is a high-tech wizard.

CASE 12 SOLUTION

Gavin uses a computer to hack into banks'
computer systems.

Case 13

THE CASE

At a meeting of his church choir, a man became flustered and irritated. It seems that he had real trouble keeping his place in the hymnal, and couldn't flip to the proper songs with adequate speed. He went home in a mood and decided he was going to do something about it. Today, choristers and others all over the world use his solution.

THE MYSTERY

What's the name of this product and its inventor?

THE CLUES

The inventor started working on this product in the 1970s.

His colleague at 3M helped him.

The product can now be found on desks and files everywhere.

Office workers are stuck on this product.

The product is often square and yellow.

CASE 13 SOLUTION

The product is a Post-It® Note, invented by Art Fry.

Case 14

THE CASE

Bob speaks fluent English (and a number of other languages), and works in a fast-food restaurant. He does not have an artificial breathing apparatus, but he lives (and breathes) comfortably at the bottom of the ocean. Each day, he and his friends visit living rooms around the world, without ever leaving the ocean floor.

THE MYSTERY

What is Bob's full name?

THE CLUES

Bob is a real animal.

Bob is a total square.

Bob's best friends are a sea star and a squid.

Bob is quite animated.

Bob knows Nick.

CASE 14 SOLUTION

Bob's full name is SpongeBob SquarePants.

Case 15

THE CASE

Wild and young Erin goes to five parties in rapid succession. She arrives home at 1:30 a.m. and collapses in a heap, exhausted, on her bed. She wakes up exactly 29 minutes later and groggily walks to the bathroom. Four minutes later she returns to bed, and realizes that it is now 3:03 a.m.

THE MYSTERY

What day of the week is it?

THE CLUES

Erin did not pass out in the bathroom.

Erin really was out of bed for only four minutes.

Erin's clocks don't show the correct time.

It's springtime.

6 months earlier it would have seemed Erin returned to bed an hour before she woke up.

CASE 15 SOLUTION

It's Sunday (and Daylight Savings Time has just begun).

THE CASE

A teenager lives in a seemingly normal town. When she goes out at night, however, she always manages to encounter evildoers. Though she is young and sometimes reluctant, she always seems to ward off the wicked in less than an hour.

THE MYSTERY

What is the girl's name and what is her night job?

THE CLUES

The girl recently graduated from high school and went to college.

The girl works nights at a very demanding job.

The girl fights evil and lives in Sunnydale.

The girl has a real stake in her classmate's safety.

The girl's best friend is named Willow.

CASE 16 SOLUTION

The girl's name is Buffy and she is a vampire slayer.

More 30 SECOND MYSTERIES

WHAT

—-—-—-—

Case 17

THE CASE

Patrick closes his eyes and ingests a large amount of a potentially fatal substance. This substance can cause nausea, vomiting, restlessness and seizures. Patrick does not need a prescription from a doctor and the substance is not marked as toxic. However, in large enough doses it may result in death. Despite this, Patrick ingests some of this substance every day at the same time.

THE MYSTERY

What is the substance and when does Patrick ingest it?

THE CLUES

The substance has no medical benefits for Patrick.

If Patrick doesn't ingest the substance, he will get headaches.

The substance is popular in Italy, Austria and the United States.

Sometimes the substance is powdered; sometimes it's liquid.

The substance is usually black or brown.

CASE 17 SOLUTION

Patrick drinks a large cup of coffee every morning.

More 30 SECOND
MYSTERIES

WHAT

– · – · · – · – · – · –

Case 18

THE CASE

Two American plumbers hear that a distant land has been conquered by hostile invaders and decide to aid the inhabitants. After arriving in the land, they encounter many strange creatures and journey through vast unexplored spaces while trying to exert control over the land and its curious resources. For their actions, they become famous.

THE MYSTERY

What are the plumbers' names and where do they travel?

THE CLUES

The plumbers' ancestors hailed from Italy.

The plumbers are brothers and look very similar.

The distant land is ruled by a beautiful woman.

The plumbers have moustaches and wear overalls.

The plumbers are fictional characters created by Nintendo®.

CASE 18SOLUTION

The plumbers are the Super Mario Bros® Mario and Luigi, who travel to the Mushroom Kingdom.

THE CASE

Ivy learns that an obese, middle-aged man needs surgery. After making thorough preparations, she carefully removes various body parts from her patient, including several major organs. He does not die and Ivy does not get in trouble.

THE MYSTERY

What does Ivy use to operate and who is the man?

THE CLUES

The man has no family or friends.

Ivy does not have a medical degree, but has been authorized to operate.

Ivy does the surgery free of charge.

Ivy has a very steady hand.

If Ivy makes a mistake, she will hear a buzz.

CASE 19 SOLUTION

Ivy is playing the game Operation®. She operates on Sam the patient with tweezers.

More 30 SECOND
MYSTERIES

WHAT

—·—·—·—·—·—

Case 20

THE CASE

A large and unsteady structure towers over a selected group of people. The group has come together because the building must be dismantled – slowly and with great skill. Against their better judgment, they begin to take it apart, hoping it will not topple in their direction.

THE MYSTERY

What is the group doing and what is the structure made of?

THE CLUES

They must make the structure taller in the process of tearing it down.

Only one person at a time can dismantle the structure, one piece at a time.

The group will probably cheer when the structure finally falls.

Those involved must extract pieces using just one hand.

Milton Bradley® built the original tower, which is made of a natural substance.

CASE 20 SOLUTION

They are playing the game Jenga® and the structure is made of wooden blocks.

WHAT

Case 21

THE CASE

Barbara has lived in the Los Angeles area all her life. She has blond hair, a curvaceous body and an incredible wardrobe. She has had a wide variety of careers, but is best known as a model. Despite her short stature she is known throughout the world.

THE MYSTERY

What is Barbara more commonly known as?

THE CLUES

Barbara was born in the 1950s.

She has had the same steady boyfriend her entire life.

Few people know if Barbara even has a last name.

Barbara is better known by her nickname.

Everyone thinks that Barbara is a real doll.

CASE 21 SOLUTION

She is known throughout the world as a Barbie® doll.

WHAT

- - ∙ - - ∙ - -

Case 22

THE CASE

In the backwoods of Europe, an older man lovingly strokes his charges. Their fat bellies protrude as they willingly gather around him at mealtime. Although he loves them, he always makes them eat much more than their fill. They don't seem to mind terribly as this is all they've ever known.

THE MYSTERY

Who is the man feeding and where will they end up?

THE CLUES

The man probably feeds them cornmeal.

The man insists that they get fatter and fatter.

When this group passes on, he can always get a new flock.

The French eat up the results.

The end product is expensive and delicious.

CASE 22 SOLUTION

The man is force-feeding geese to make foie gras (or goose liver pate); these geese will end up on someone's plate.

THE CASE

From her designated spot, Josey watches people all day. She stares right at them, without looking away and they mostly pretend not to see her. If she feels like it, she might follow a few people around to get a better idea of what they're up to.

THE MYSTERY

What is Josey doing and why aren't people bothered by it?

THE CLUES

Josey is not crazy or homeless.

Josey gets paid to watch people carefully.

Josey's clothes are monochromatic.

Josey works with a partner.

Josey is fond of donuts.

CASE 23 SOLUTION

Josey watches people while she works as a police officer; no one minds because she's just doing her job.

THE CASE

A room contains a large square surrounded by a group of people. One by one the people approach the center of the square and throw their bodies into strange positions. All intend to maintain their stance, but after time many grow weak, collapse in a heap and are forced to leave the square.

THE MYSTERY

What are they doing and why are they doing it?

THE CLUES

The people are all adults.

They are not involved in a protest or doing yoga.

They keep their clothes on the whole time.

Sometimes they use their feet, other times they use their hands.

The square is covered in giant, colored polka dots.

CASE 24 SOLUTION

They are playing the game Twister® because it is fun.

More 30 SECOND
MYSTERIES

WHAT

—·—·—·—·—·—

Case 25

THE CASE

Bill is at a desk in a large corporation when – without warning – someone grabs him and forces him into a dark bag. After a full night's journey, he is dropped off in New York by a uniformed stranger.

THE MYSTERY

What type of company does Bill work for and what's the name of the uniformed stranger's company?

THE CLUES

Bill is very important to his company's success.

Bill's company makes life easier for many people—but also gets people into trouble.

The stranger works for the U.S. government and makes deliveries for a living.

Bill's company gives its clients real credit for working with them.

Bill is not a real person and gets sent out every month!

CASE 25 SOLUTION

Bill works for a credit card company. The uniformed stranger works for the U.S. Postal Service.

More 30 SECOND
MYSTERIES
WHAT

Case 26

THE CASE

Mary straps her son Nicholas into a machine and then casually turns it on. After a series of explosions, Mary turns off the machine, unstraps Nicholas and leaves the machine behind. Neither Mary, Nicholas, nor the machine are harmed.

THE MYSTERY

What did Mary use to turn on the machine and what type of machine is it?

THE CLUES

Mary is not an engineer.

Mary owns the machine.

The explosions are mechanically controlled and are perfectly normal.

The device used to turn on the machine can be held in Mary's hand.

Mary bought the machine at her local Ford dealership.

CASE 26 SOLUTION

Mary used a key to turn on her car.

Case 27

THE CASE

Groups of men desperate for jobs converge on a site. Immediately, they are put to work digging, blasting and hauling. They endure sweltering temperatures and poor sanitary conditions to make their meager wages. When their massive project is finished, it is the largest of its kind anywhere in the world.

THE MYSTERY

What did these men help build and where can it be found?

THE CLUES

Six of the largest construction companies in the country worked together to build it.

It was first built to help irrigate an arid region.

FDR dedicated the completed project in 1935.

It stands more than 700 feet high.

It stops the mighty Colorado River.

CASE 27 SOLUTION

They built the Hoover Dam; it lies on the boundary between southeast Nevada and northwest Arizona.

THE CASE

Lorraine's foreign language teacher is never absent and is always in a good mood. She even takes Lorraine and a bunch of other kids on a field trip every day of the week. They all practice their foreign language skills while learning how to read a map, make new friends and stay away from foxes.

THE MYSTERY

What language is Lorraine learning and who is her teacher?

THE CLUES

The teacher always brings a backpack.
They often visit the teacher's abuela.
The teacher has her own TV show.
She has a dark brown bob haircut and big brown eyes.
The teacher is a child.

CASE 28 SOLUTION

Lorraine's teacher is Dora the Explorer™. She teaches Spanish.

WHERE

More 30 SECOND
MYSTERIES

WHERE

—··—··—··—

Case 1

THE CASE

Audrey steps into a long, enclosed area. Suddenly and without warning, spherical objects come hurtling towards her at great speeds. She could easily escape, but instead chooses to brandish a weapon of sorts and attempt to actually attack the objects. Friends and family stand by and shout encouragement, but do nothing to help her get out of harm's way.

THE MYSTERY

Where is Audrey and what is she doing?

THE CLUES

Audrey actually paid money to experience this abuse.

Some might call this "practice."

Audrey has been called a real swinger.

She attacks the objects with a long wooden piece of equipment.

Her favorite team is the Yankees.

CASE 1 SOLUTION

Audrey is in a batting cage, hitting baseballs and practicing her swing.

THE CASE

Mr. Blaine lives in Africa and runs a small eating and drinking establishment, which has become a local tourist trap. One night he is asked by a wanted man to protect a valuable possession. Moments later the man is murdered and Mr. Blaine's life falls into turmoil. The police do not arrest Mr. Blaine, despite his guilt in committing numerous crimes.

THE MYSTERY

Where is Mr. Blaine's business and what is it called?

THE CLUES

Mr. Blaine lives in Northern Africa, where most people speak French.

Mr. Blain's story is told in a movie.

World War II is raging during Mr. Blaine's time.

Mr. Blaine named his café after himself.

The valuable possession includes letters of transit to Lisbon.

CASE 2 SOLUTION

Mr. Blaine's business, Rick's Café, is located in Morocco.

WHERE

-·-·-·-·-·-

Case 3

THE CASE

A huge outdoor sign is raised to draw attention to new real estate. The sign costs $21,000, but is less than 20 letters long. Although it is only meant to advertise the prime property for a year and a half, it remains in the same location for eight decades.

THE MYSTERY

Where is the sign located and what does it say?

THE CLUES

The property being advertised is in wooded hills overlooking a downtown area.

The sign was erected in 1923.

The sign is over 50 feet tall and each letter is over 30 feet wide.

The sign is built on the side of Mt. Lee.

The sign has become a landmark of the movie-making capital of the world.

CASE 3 SOLUTION

The Hollywood sign is located in the Hollywood area of Los Angeles, CA.

THE CASE

A travel-worn and slightly grubby woman walks into an establishment and immediately takes off some of her outerwear. When she does this, the shop workers get down on the ground. After about 30 minutes, she leaves the business but the workers remain crouched near the floor.

THE MYSTERY

Where is this woman and why did she go to the shop?

THE CLUES

The workers are not afraid of her.

They do this kind of thing for every client.

Sitting down low keeps them closer to the object of their labors.

The woman read a magazine while being serviced.

The woman is seeking a more "polished" look.

CASE 4 SOLUTION

The woman is in a salon, getting a pedicure from trained pedicurists.

More 30 SECOND
MYSTERIES

WHERE

-- - -- - -- - -- - --

Case 5

THE CASE

Dorothy is driving outside in an open space. Her speed is over 100 mph. There are people standing all around her, remarking on her fast driving. She isn't concerned that she will hit anyone and no one is concerned about being run over, although some are standing within a few feet of her.

THE MYSTERY

Where is Dorothy and why aren't people worried about being hit?

THE CLUES

If Dorothy were to hit anyone, the impact could kill or seriously injure the person.
Although her driving is fast, Dorothy would say that she's taking her time.
When Dorothy drives she actually ends up walking.
The people watching are not in Dorothy's direct path.
Dorothy is participating in a competition, but she's not at a racetrack.

CASE 5 SOLUTION

Dorothy is at a golf tournament. People aren't worried because Dorothy is hitting a golf ball, which is also known as "driving."

More 30 SECOND
MYSTERIES
WHERE

Case 6

THE CASE

Kai and Trevor sit down to discuss their plans. As soon as Trevor takes a seat, Kai leaps into the air. Trevor tries to get him to return to the discussion, but Kai just can't get himself settled on the ground. However, when Trevor gets up off of his seat, Kai suddenly slams to the ground unharmed.

THE MYSTERY

Where are Kai and Trevor and why did Kai leap into the air?

THE CLUES

Kai is sitting down the entire time.

Both Kai and Trevor are less than 8 years old.

Kai and Trevor face each other while they talk.

Kai went into the air because Trevor sat down.

Trevor weighs much more than Kai.

CASE 6 SOLUTION

Kai and Trevor are at a playground when Kai gets stuck at the top of the see-saw because he's much lighter than Trevor.

MYSTERIES

WHERE

—·—·—·—·—·—

Case 7

THE CASE

Georgia's professional life is on the edge. Georgia goes to work in the dark and spends her time feeling hot while she goes about her business. She is constantly being visited by truck drivers who want to touch her buns and chat with her while she works. Georgia never raises her voice and often thanks the men for dropping by.

THE MYSTERY

Where does Georgia work and why does she thank the truck drivers?

THE CLUES

Georgia often offers the truck drivers a creamy surprise.

Georgia's customers start arriving about three hours after Georgia.

Georgia's buns aren't attached to her body.

The truck drivers are delivering important materials for Georgia.

Georgia is hot because she is surrounded by ovens all day.

CASE 7 SOLUTION

Georgia works in a bakery. She thanks the truck drivers for their business.

Case 8

THE CASE

Leslie is a college student who is notified by her university that she can't attend school in September 2006. Her grades are excellent and she is current on all school fees. Not only is Leslie not welcome but there will be no professors or students at the school until 2007. Leslie is notified that she can attend another school for the rest of the calendar year.

THE MYSTERY

Where does Leslie go to school and why can't she return?

THE CLUES

Although this is an extremely rare event, Leslie is not completely surprised.
The university wants Leslie to return in 2007.
The events that led to the university's decision were not under its control.
Many other institutions in the area were also closed for a number of months.
When the event occurred, Louisiana declared a state of emergency.

CASE 8 SOLUTION

Leslie attends Tulane University, which was devastated by Hurricane Katrina in 2006. The university was closed while New Orleans was rebuilt, so students attended other schools.

Case 9

THE CASE

A woman, with no medical or psychological training, spends each night talking to strangers who come to visit her. She regularly dispenses mood-altering drugs and listens to the strangers' problems.

THE MYSTERY

Where does the woman work and what is her occupation?

THE CLUES

Some strangers don't want to talk but are still anxious for her attention.

Many strangers want to talk to her at the same time.

The strangers tend to become more talkative the longer they are there.

Many of the strangers return regularly.

The strangers tend to drink, but not because they are thirsty.

CASE 9 SOLUTION

The woman works in a bar as a bartender.

Case 10

THE CASE

Sam spends his days in a small room with very sharp objects, electrical devices and an assortment of liquids. Every 30 minutes, Sam attacks another person, but he never gets arrested. Surprisingly, when Sam physically touches his victims they never scream, and when he cuts them they rarely bleed.

THE MYSTERY

Where does Sam spend his days and why don't the victims complain?

THE CLUES

People actually line up to have Sam attack them.

People talk to Sam while he works.

People return every month or two.

Sam likes to sit when he's not working.

Sam's victims pay Sam for his service.

CASE 10 SOLUTION

Sam spends his days in his barbershop. His "victims" are happy with the haircuts he gives them.

Case 11

THE CASE

A group of adventurers find themselves trapped. There are high, steep walls on either side and they are surrounded by water. The group is traveling at high speeds without jet propulsion or a motor. They are inches away from death, yet they continue to keep moving.

THE MYSTERY

Where is the group and what are they doing?

THE CLUES

The group is in a southwestern state in the United States.

The group is traveling on the water.

The high steep walls define a national landmark.

Many groups have traveled here before and survived.

The group is on the Colorado River.

CASE 11 SOLUTION

The group is rafting through the Grand Canyon.

Case 12

THE CASE

After a long night of travel, Pierre finds himself in a strange land. He does not recognize any of the words that the people are speaking as he wanders around. He does see lots of water, lots of shops and a beautiful mermaid.

THE MYSTERY

Where is Pierre?

THE CLUES

Pierre is in Europe.

Pierre traveled by train.

Pierre started in France.

The land Pierre ended in was Hans Christian Andersen's home.

The mermaid that Pierre saw is a statue.

CASE 12 SOLUTION

Pierre is in Copenhagen, where the famous "Little Mermaid" statue sits by the bay.

Case 13

THE CASE

A man from the Dominican Republic, weighing more than 100 kilos and measuring more than 74 inches, fits snugly into a box. Then he grabs a stick and sends a spherical object toward a green-colored monster. The monster doesn't seem to notice, but a loud thunder erupts.

THE MYSTERY

Where is the man and what is his name?

THE CLUES

The man is at a sporting event.

The man was called a World Champion in 2004.

The man is a professional athlete in Boston.

The man is more offensive than defensive.

The man is known as Big Papi.

CASE 13 SOLUTION

The man is in Fenway Park. His name is David Ortiz and he is a Designated Hitter for the Boston Red Sox. The crowd erupts in thunderous applause when he hits a home run over the left-field wall, or "Green Monster."

THE CASE

"Ooh, look at all of that blood!" screams Eve. Steve looks forward about 30 yards and smiles. This is his kind of night. He doesn't try to help or call for the police. He just sits and smiles along with thousands of others as the massacre continues. The victim is shirtless, with a cut above his eye and a broken nose. The unarmed predator leaves the scene without any interference.

THE MYSTERY

Where are Steve and Eve and why does the predator get to leave?

THE CLUES

Steve and Eve knew what time the massacre would begin.

Everyone witnessing the attack paid money to see it.

Neither the victim nor the attacker are bare handed.

The attack was promoted as a sporting event.

A winner was declared and celebrated by all in attendance.

CASE 14 SOLUTION

Steve and Eve are at a boxing match. The "predator" leaves after winning the bout.

THE CASE

Every morning Tricia walks five blocks and enters a government building where she stays for 7 hours. Each day Mr. Smith, a government employee, makes physical contact with Tricia. He never says anything and doesn't know Tricia's name. At day's end, Mr. Smith always smiles as he sees her coming. While never convicted, he is an admitted interdigitator. Tricia isn't frightened by Mr. Smith and doesn't report him to the authorities.

THE MYSTERY

Where does Mr. Smith work and what does he do for a living?

THE CLUES

Tricia is 6 years old.

Mr. Smith works for the public school district.

Mr. Smith works outdoors.

Tricia doesn't know how to cross the street by herself.

Mr. Smith is in the safety business.

CASE 15 SOLUTION

Mr. Smith is a crossing guard at the local school.

THE CASE

The water woke Max up when it hit his mouth. He did not know how long he had been asleep. Max was miles from home and he had no idea how he would return since he didn't have his car keys or any money on him. Dressed only in his boxers, he had no recollection of taking off his clothes, which were nowhere to be found.

THE MYSTERY

Where was Max and what happened to his belongings?

THE CLUES

Max was not crazy or ill.

Max had not been in an accident, but he had been celebrating his 21st birthday.

The water had a salty taste.

Max lived in Hawaii.

The tide had come in and gone out again.

CASE 16 SOLUTION

Max fell asleep on the beach and his clothes floated away.

Case 17

THE CASE

A wildly charismatic individual convinces a small group of people to join his exclusive club. Being a member means you have to adhere to certain rules and always listen to the director's instructions. These guidelines involve acts that some would deem downright crazy, but the members do them anyway.

THE MYSTERY

Where is the leader of this group now and what is his name?

THE CLUES

Group members would do anything to keep their "boss" happy.

The family wasn't afraid of blood and guts.

Murder and mayhem were their calling cards.

Sharon Tate fell victim to this group.

The Beatles wrote the song "Helter Skelter" about this man and his followers.

CASE 17 SOLUTION

The group leader, Charles Manson, is now in jail.

WHERE

Case 18

THE CASE

A photographer witnesses a murder and manages to shoot some pictures of the crime. The photos show the prime suspect in the case and match the detailed descriptions from other witnesses. The suspect has an airtight alibi and tells the police where to find the real murderer.

THE MYSTERY

Where did the police find the murderer and how did the suspect know the murderer?

THE CLUES

The suspect was very familiar with the spot where the murderer was found.

The suspect knew the murderer very well.

The suspect was reluctant to turn in the murderer.

The police found the murderer where he lived.

The suspect and the murderer were born on the same day—and live in the same house.

CASE 18 SOLUTION

The police found the murderer in his home. The suspect and the murderer were identical twins who lived with their parents.

Case 19

THE CASE

On December 23rd, Amy boards a commercial airliner in New York bound for San Francisco. She takes her seat and stows her briefcase in the overhead compartment. The plane does not deviate from its flight plan and makes no unscheduled stops. When the plane reaches its final destination, Amy and her briefcase are no longer on the plane.

THE MYSTERY

Where did Amy end up and how did she get off the plane?

THE CLUES

Amy did not have a parachute.

Amy never left the U.S. and never crossed the Rocky Mountains.

Amy's hometown is a Midwestern city, known for its arch.

Amy stood up and walked quickly to the front of the plane in a normal manner.

Amy's husband met her at the airport gate and drove her home.

CASE 19 SOLUTION

Amy walked down the jetway when the plane made its scheduled stop in St. Louis.

THE CASE

A young blonde scientist is dropped on the shores of a foreign country. She lives in a tent and befriends a native with a white beard named David. She lives in the same community as his family for many years but never really feels like a relative.

THE MYSTERY

Where is the woman and what is her name?

THE CLUES

The woman is from England.

This meeting took place in the 1960s.

David eats bananas.

The woman is a famous anthropologist.

The woman now fights to protect David and his kind.

CASE 20 SOLUTION

The woman is Jane Goodall and David is David Greybeard, a chimpanzee.

Case 21

THE CASE

As a shop owner locks up for the night, an elderly man jumps out from behind a parked car, stabs the owner several times and sprints down the street. George witnesses the crime from two blocks away, but does not cry for help or call the police.

THE MYSTERY

Where is George and what is he doing?

THE CLUES

George knows the shop owner very well.

The elderly man is actually in his late 40s.

The shop owner is neither dead nor hurt.

There are over 20 other witnesses to the crime, all of whom are working.

George employs both the shop owner and the elderly man.

CASE 21 SOLUTION

George is on a movie set directing a horror flick.

Case 22

THE CASE

A woman goes to see the same man every week for several years. She tells him her deepest secrets. She tells him things she wouldn't even tell her best friend, yet she can't get herself to look him in the eye. She values his advice, but never tells him her name.

THE MYSTERY

Where does she visit the man and why is she so intent on talking to him?

THE CLUES

The man wears a uniform.

The man has many other visitors, but most visit very infrequently.

Both the woman and the man have a tendency to repeat things.

The woman feels guilty if she misses their meeting.

A wall and a covered window separate the woman and the man.

CASE 22 SOLUTION

The woman goes to church to visit her priest every week for confession.

More 30 SECOND MYSTERIES

WHERE

- - - - - - - -

Case 23

THE CASE

An enterprising young illustrator makes commercially successful drawings for the masses. Although he is respected for this work, he really gets noticed when he starts stealing ideas and designs from others. No one minds his pilfering ways; in fact, he becomes a revered and often imitated sensation.

THE MYSTERY

Where did the illustrator work and what are his most recognizable images?

THE CLUES

He didn't make some of the work that bears his name.

Even though he was highly intelligent, he rarely gave a coherent interview.

Groupies surrounded him nearly all the time.

He made the most of his "15 minutes of fame."

Liz Taylor and Jackie O. appear over and over in his work.

CASE 23 SOLUTION

Andy Warhol worked at The Factory in New York. His Campbell soup can prints are probably his most famous pieces.

Case 24

THE CASE

Four reddened individuals walk to the edge of a hole, where they stop and lethargically gaze in. Vertigo threatens to ruin the experience, so they look out at the rocks before them. Soon, they mount animals and begin their grueling descent.

THE MYSTERY

Where are the people and what is the geological entity?

THE CLUES

Humans have lived near it for around 4,000 years.

Astronauts have reported seeing it from space.

It's a family vacation hot spot.

The landmark has been a national park since 1919.

It's located in Arizona.

CASE 24 SOLUTION

The people are riding burrows into the Grand Canyon.

Case 25

THE CASE

A man arrives at his workplace, ready to wait on his first customer. When she arrives, both shoulders are covered with dirt and she smells horrible. Suddenly, she begins kicking the man with all his might. They struggle until the man finally manages to lock her in the back room and leave the office.

THE MYSTERY

Where is the man and what was he doing?

THE CLUES

The man's home is adjacent to his workplace.

The man sees the same customers every day.

The man wears overalls to work.

The man's first customer is "udderly" feminine.

The man works seven days a week.

CASE 25 SOLUTION

The man is on a dairy farm and he is milking cows.

Case 26

THE CASE

Sonya leans over a younger girl who is confined to a chair. As the girl screams in anguish, Sonya cuts off a piece of the girl's body and throws it to the floor. This makes the girl's cries even more desperate, but Sonya just ignores them and continues. Finally, Sonya takes a hot piece of metal and continually scorches a body part of the little girl.

THE MYSTERY

Where is Sonya and why is the little girl crying?

THE CLUES

Sonya does this several times a day.

The girl is not restrained, but she can't get up from the chair until Sonya is done.

The young girl's mother paid Sonya to do this to her.

The girl is not in physical pain.

The little girl likes her hair long.

CASE 26 SOLUTION

Sonya is in a hair salon where she is cutting and curling the hair of a reluctant young girl.

More 30 SECOND
MYSTERIES

WHERE

—·—·—·—·—·—·—

Case 27

THE CASE

On the riverfront of a great city, a dream starts. Distinguished individuals from many regions want to contribute, but in the end only one person gets his way. Minions arrive and begin the difficult process of creating the man's dream. It is thought that many will die making it, yet all survive to see the project completed and reach its majestic height.

THE MYSTERY

Where is the structure and what is it called?

THE CLUES

It's considered a feat of engineering.

The final section was wedged into place in 1965.

It was designed to last 1,000 years.

From the top, visitors can see Illinois to the east and Missouri to the west.

It is a 630-foot tall arched monument to Westward expansion.

CASE 27 SOLUTION

It is St. Louis' Gateway Arch; it was built to commemorate the opening of the American West in the 1800s.

More 30 SECOND
MYSTERIES

WHERE

—.—.—.—.—.—

Case 28

THE CASE

Clint and Joel have prepared for a certain event months in advance, but some other men have not prepared at all. A gun is fired and while no one is shot, thousands of people scramble forward. They fight each other to take things that belong to the U.S. government, but no action is taken against them. Some people cheat and later become famous for it.

THE MYSTERY

Where did this event take place?

THE CLUES

The event is not a game.

The event takes place in the Mid-West.

The year is 1906.

Clint and Joel are in a real rush and hope to land on their feet.

The cheaters are known as Sooners.

CASE 28 SOLUTION

The event is the Oklahoma Land Rush and it took place in Oklahoma.

WHY

More 30 SECOND
MYSTERIES

WHY

Case 1

THE CASE

11 big angry men skip church and walk onto an empty field one February Sunday.
All of the men work in Massachusetts, but they have congregated in New Orleans to
conquer a western adversary. After less than three hours, they are victorious and
host a national celebration.

THE MYSTERY

Why are the men in New Orleans and by what name are they better known?

THE CLUES

The men work together 6 months each year in the Fall.
The men defeated many foes to have the opportunity to challenge the adversary.
The event will be the most-watched event of the year.
The men refer to themselves using a name that refers to the American Revolution.
When the men win they are declared World Champions.

CASE 1 SOLUTION

In February 2002, the New England Patriots football team defeated the St. Louis Rams in Super Bowl XXXVI, which was held in New Orleans.

THE CASE

Connie is a huge football fan. She never answers the phone while a game is on, and her friends know not to interrupt her. One Sunday, she sits down with her family to watch her favorite team play its arch rival. Connie's family notices she already seems to know the outcome of the game, then she correctly tells them the final score . . . in advance.

THE MYSTERY

Why did Connie know the score in advance?

THE CLUES

Connie is not a psychic.

The game is not fixed.

Connie knows the final score with absolute certainty.

Connie did not have access to a computer.

The game was played on Sunday morning.

CASE 2 SOLUTION

Connie taped the game earlier in the day and had already watched the end when she sat down to watch it with her family.

More 30 SECOND
MYSTERIES

WHY

–·–·–·–·–·–

Case 3

THE CASE

Courtney and Mike sit down to dinner in a nice restaurant that serves their favorite kind of food. They place their orders and enjoy their soup while waiting for the main course. When the waiter brings their meals, they notice that the meat is extremely uncooked, but they proceed to have a wonderful meal anyway.

THE MYSTERY

Why didn't Courtney and Mike care that their meat wasn't cooked?

THE CLUES

Their soup contains chopped scallions.

Courtney and Mike count rice as one of their favorite foods.

The restaurant is known for its seafood.

Courtney and Mike like to use chopsticks when they eat.

Their meal was served with soy sauce.

CASE 3 SOLUTION

Courtney and Mike ordered sushi.

THE CASE

Mel is a model who is preparing to audition for a lucrative photo shoot. The model who is chosen will pose in the shoot immediately after the audition. The model will have a number of close-ups, so a smooth shave with no cuts is essential. But Mel draws blood while shaving, and ends up with two deep gashes covered by two scabs. Nonetheless, Mel is chosen, and earns the big bucks.

THE MYSTERY

Why was Mel chosen?

THE CLUES

Mel is a well-known model.

Mel has a particular specialty.

Mel is a nickname.

The photographer will not shoot Mel's whole body.

The cuts were on Mel's underarms.

CASE 4 SOLUTION

Mel is a "leg" model and the cuts were not on her legs.

THE CASE

Herbie lives at sea level, near the beach. The temperature where he lives can get as high as 95° in the summer. Although it's July and the temperature is at its monthly high, Herbie is quite cold and wears sweaters and gloves.

THE MYSTERY

Why is Herbie cold?

THE CLUES

Herbie is healthy and has normal blood circulation.

Herbie always wears warm clothing in July.

Everyone around Herbie is wearing warm clothing, too.

To some, Herbie might seem upside down.

Herbie has a particular accent.

CASE 5 SOLUTION

*Herbie lives in Australia, where July is a
winter month.*

THE CASE

Free divers stay underwater for as long as they can on a single breath of air. Competitive free divers train for months by lifting weights, running and practicing yoga. The current world record is nearly 9 minutes. Although Barbara has never trained to be a free diver, she routinely stays underwater for days at a time.

THE MYSTERY

Why can Barbara stay underwater for so long?

THE CLUES

Barbara is in good shape, but she is not an exceptional athlete.

Barbara can't hold her breath for much longer than 1 minute.

Barbara does not hold her breath while she's underwater.

Other people are with Barbara while she is underwater.

Barbara is in the Navy, but she's not a frogman (or frogwoman)!

CASE 6 SOLUTION

Barbara is stationed on a submarine.

More 30 SECOND
MYSTERIES

WHY

Case 7

THE CASE

While performing one of his daily tasks at the hospital, Dr. Mendelsohn asks a uniformed woman standing next to the table to hand him an item. He knows that she is not a trained medical professional and that there are several qualified nurses sitting idly nearby. When the woman hands him the wrong item, Dr. Mendelsohn takes it anyway and says it will do.

THE MYSTERY

Why does Dr. Mendelsohn go to the untrained woman for help and in what department of the hospital does the doctor perform this task?

THE CLUES

The woman has worked for the hospital for 15 years, but she's never administered a shot.

She doesn't work for Dr. Mendelsohn, but helps him nearly every day.

Although she has no medical training, she's assisted thousands of patients, physicians and nurses.

Before the doctor leaves, the woman hands him a bill for $8.95.

The doctor sees this woman to have his nutritional needs fulfilled.

CASE 7 SOLUTION

The doctor is ordering his breakfast from a waitress at the hospital cafeteria.

THE CASE

Bob loves to solve mysteries, and he's quite good at it. In one week, he solves more mysteries than Sherlock Holmes did in his entire (fictional) career. Even though he identifies murderers, solves crimes and locates stolen property, no one is sent to jail. Nonetheless, Bob is thoroughly satisfied and looking forward to solving more mysteries.

THE MYSTERY

Why is Bob so satisfied?

THE CLUES

Bob is not an actor.

Bob does not work for the police department.

Bob solves mysteries on his own time.

Bob pays money for the chance to solve mysteries.

Bob loves to play games and read books.

CASE 8 SOLUTION

Bob is playing 30 Second Mysteries.

THE CASE

Jack Hammer creeps cautiously through a smoldering block of burnt-out buildings, gripping his machine gun tightly. Sirens wail, searchlights search and the sounds of explosions fill the night air. Suddenly, a grenade explodes two feet from Jack and, from his perspective, everything fades to black. Jack is killed instantaneously. A moment later, Jack stands up and dejectedly walks into his kitchen to get a glass of water.

THE MYSTERY

Why could Jack get up after he died?

THE CLUES

Jack knew that he would die long before the grenade exploded.

Jack looked forward to fighting, even though he knew the outcome.

Jack has died many times before.

Despite the violence in this scene, no one was hurt.

Jack was holding something in his hands, but it wasn't a machine gun.

CASE 9 SOLUTION

Jack was playing a video game.

More 30 SECOND
MYSTERIES

WHY

– · – · – · – · –

Case 10

THE CASE

Zack sits on a stool surrounded by his possessions, many of which are family heirlooms. Strangers come by and take his belongings, some without ever uttering a word to him. He is sad to see many of his possessions disappear, but doesn't complain or try to get his things back.

THE MYSTERY

Why is Zack surrounded by his possessions and why does he let people take them?

THE CLUES

Though this isn't his job, Zack is getting paid for what he's doing.

Zack hopes that nothing will be left at the end of the day.

If any of the items are left, Zack could always put them in his garage.

The people who come by are responding to an ad that Zack placed in the newspaper.

Zack is accepting money for the items.

CASE 10 SOLUTION

Zack is having a garage sale.

More 30 SECOND
MYSTERIES

WHY

— · — · — · — · —

Case 11

THE CASE

Buzz is sent into a barrage of bombs and gunfire with no protective armor besides a standard issue helmet. He is in constant danger, but he never once raises his gun against the enemy. Instead, he shoots several of his own country's soldiers. He later receives a medal for bravery in battle.

THE MYSTERY

Why does Buzz shoot his own countrymen and why does he receive a medal for bravery?

THE CLUES

Buzz has never gone through boot camp.

He is paid to shoot his fellow countrymen.

The soldiers he shot were not injured.

Buzz is not a mercenary but his job takes him from one war to another.

Buzz's work brings the war to his countrymen.

CASE 11 SOLUTION

Buzz is a war photographer who bravely goes into battle to shoot pictures of soldiers at war.

Case 12

THE CASE

It's Saturday and Jane is alone working on her computer at one end of a large office. Dick runs into the office at the other end and shouts, "Fire!" Jane keeps on working. Jane continues to work peacefully, ignoring Dick completely. Finally, Dick reaches Jane, taps her on the shoulder and pulls her out of her seat. They run to safety.

THE MYSTERY

Why did Jane ignore Dick's attempts to help her?

THE CLUES

Jane was glad to have Dick's help.

Dick did not know Jane.

Had Jane looked up and seen Dick, she would have known that something was wrong.

Jane did not realize that Dick was there.

Jane has trouble speaking.

CASE 12 SOLUTION

Jane is deaf.

THE CASE

Many people are gathered and separated into two distinctive groups. The people in one group are all wearing matching clothes and the people in the other group are spectators. Everyone will leave once the first group has taken off an article of clothing and thrown it as far as they can.

THE MYSTERY

Why are these people gathered and which article of clothing will be thrown?

THE CLUES

The crowd is full of young and old people alike.

Many of the people are crying.

It's an important day for the people who are all dressed alike.

The crowd is made up mostly of friends and family.

The people dressed alike are wearing robes.

CASE 13 SOLUTION

It is a graduation ceremony and the graduates will throw their caps into the air.

More 30 SECOND MYSTERIES

WHY

–·–··–··–·–·–

Case 14

THE CASE

Julia hasn't eaten in more than a month. She is 5'3" and under 100 pounds. She spends most of her time sitting in a corner sleeping. People come to visit her, but she never says anything to them. Sometimes people bring her food, but she's not allowed to have it. The city is aware of what's going on but do nothing to stop it.

THE MYSTERY

Why doesn't Julia eat and where can she be found?

THE CLUES

Julia is not able to leave her home.

Some people visit Julia to take pictures of her beauty.

Many people take one look at Julia and scream in terror.

Julia is very healthy and well cared for.

Julia's caretakers are the only ones allowed to give her food.

CASE 14 SOLUTION

Julia is a boa constrictor in a zoo. Sometimes snakes will go long periods of time without eating.

THE CASE

It is late on Halloween and Sally enters her home. She searches the house, but her parents and younger brothers are nowhere to be found. As she enters the dark living room, she hears a voice say that he is coming to get her. Sally doesn't call the cops or leave the house and is not frightened or alarmed.

THE MYSTERY

Why isn't Sally afraid of the voice and where is it coming from?

THE CLUES

Sally is 13 years old and is scared of being home alone.

Her parents told her they'd be home when she got back from trick-or-treating with her friends.

The person whose voice Sally hears knows she's alone and knows where she lives.

The voice is coming from a machine.

The rest of her family lost track of time while trick-or-treating.

CASE 15 SOLUTION

Sally isn't afraid because the voice is on her answering machine. Her dad is letting her know that they are coming home to pick her up.

More 30 SECOND
MYSTERIES

WHY

—·—·—·—·—·—·—

Case 16

THE CASE

A man speeds off in his car. After driving for a brief period, he suddenly steers the car off a high cliff, destroying it. There are numerous witnesses to this dangerous act, but no one is upset by it.

THE MYSTERY

Why did the man crash the car and who is he?

THE CLUES

The man was not unhappy or suicidal.

The man has done similar things before.

The man was not injured, and did not expect to be.

While crashing the car, the man is pretending to be someone else.

The man's actions were recorded on camera.

CASE 16 SOLUTION

The man is a stuntman, who crashed the car for a movie scene.

Case 17

THE CASE

A family of four is relaxing in their home. Suddenly, a giant prehistoric creature invades their living room. The two children shout when they see the creature and enter a trance-like state. The parents flee the room, leaving the children alone with the creature.

THE MYSTERY

Why do the parents leave the room and what is the creature's official name?

THE CLUES

The creature stands upright on two legs.

The creature can communicate with children.

The parents know that the creature will leave within an hour.

The parents are not afraid of the creature, but are not amused by it either.

The creature is purple and enters homes throughout the U.S. simultaneously.

CASE 17 SOLUTION

The parents leave the room because Barney bores them.

THE CASE

Jenny is moving into her new apartment. The place is filthy and there are cobwebs everywhere. As she prepares her first meal in the kitchen, she finds a mouse in her box of canned goods. Jenny calmly removes the mouse and continues cooking, not bothering to wash her hands or call the landlord.

THE MYSTERY

Why isn't Jenny worried about the mouse and how did it get into her box of canned food?

THE CLUES

The mouse didn't eat any of Jenny's food.

When Jenny's cat saw the mouse, it didn't pay it any attention.

Jenny brought the mouse over from her previous apartment.

The mouse is clean and free of any diseases.

Jenny packed up her belongings in a rush when moving out of her previous apartment.

CASE 18 SOLUTION

Jenny isn't worried because the mouse is for her computer. It was misplaced during the move.

THE CASE

Andy wakes up early one morning and drives to a local school. Once inside he patiently waits. When his turn comes Andy walks into a small curtained room. He then punches away for about 10 minutes. When he finishes Andy feels triumphant, walks to his car and drives away without a scratch on him.

THE MYSTERY

Why did Andy go to the school and what was he punching?

THE CLUES

It was a November morning in 2000.

Andy does not have any children attending the school.

The school was only a temporary place for punching.

The punching involved a piece of paper.

Andy is a U.S. citizen.

CASE 19 SOLUTION

Andy was at the school to vote in an election.

More 30 SECOND
MYSTERIES

WHY

Case 20

THE CASE

Alvin is a healthy young man with no major health problems. One day as he's driving to work, something repeatedly happens to his body that causes his heart to stop. Each attack is so violent that he is unable to open his eyes whenever it occurs. When he recovers, he continues driving as if nothing had happened.

THE MYSTERY

What is happening to Alvin and why does he continue to drive in a carefree manner?

THE CLUES

Alvin is only able to keep one hand on the wheel during each attack.

The attacks force Alvin to make a loud, strange noise.

Alvin feels like his brain is coming out of his nose.

Alvin's heart only stops for a second each time he is attacked.

Alvin's car is very dusty.

CASE 20 SOLUTION

Alvin is attacked by a sneezing fit; he can continue driving because sneezing is quick and practically harmless.

THE CASE

An excited crowd lines the street, waiting impatiently for the main event. They shuffle their feet and gaze about anxiously, arching their necks for a better view. Moments later, before they catch sight of the event they've come to witness, they all quickly scatter. They know there is no real danger, but quickly give up their prized curbside spots and run for cover anyway.

THE MYSTERY

Why has the crowd gathered and what makes them run for cover?

THE CLUES

There are lots of families in the crowd.

What occurred is completely natural.

They are in a city or town.

The sky above them became dark.

The performers – and the on-lookers – probably got wet.

CASE 21 SOLUTION

---

*The crowd has gathered to watch a parade; they run
for cover because it starts to rain.*

THE CASE

Mary is a well-known artist. To celebrate her big exhibition, she uses her best brushes, oils and pencils to paint herself. It takes her a long time to perfect her work, but when she steps back to admire what she's done, she is very proud. No one seems to notice these latest efforts during the show, but Mary still feels the night was a big success.

THE MYSTERY

Why doesn't anyone pay attention to Mary's latest work and why doesn't this bother her?

THE CLUES

Whenever someone tells Mary that she looks nice, she changes the topic.

Mary bought her pencils and brushes at the mall.

Mary most often works with clay or chisels.

Mary required a crew of people to carry her work into the gallery.

Mary wanted to look her best for the exhibition.

CASE 22 SOLUTION

Mary is a sculptor who "painted" her face with makeup in preparation for her show. She is happy that people notice her sculptures instead of her face.

THE CASE

Jim peers into a small window and observes a British family having a serious discussion. Jim is one of many people anonymously spying on the family. The family discusses personal business and inevitably engages in a heated argument. Within 30 minutes, Jim's view of the family is obscured. He knows that there is a possibility of violence, but doesn't call the police. Instead, he leaves the area and makes a mental note to return in seven days and take another peek at the family.

THE MYSTERY

Why doesn't the family care that Jim is spying on them?

THE CLUES

The family is constantly surrounded by people.

The family lives in California.

Jim likes to watch MTV.

The family is wealthy.

The dad is a (bleeping) rock star.

CASE 23 SOLUTION

The family is the Osbournes and they are on MTV.

THE CASE

The victim of a mugging picks Frank "The Hammer" Pelligrino out of a police line-up. Frank is well-known by the police and is reputed to know a great deal about this mugging and a host of other criminal activities such as prostitution, drugs and illegal gambling. However, Frank has strong connections to a powerful organization and he is released without charges being filed.

THE MYSTERY

Why is Frank allowed to go free and what organization does he work for?

THE CLUES

The victim had seen Frank at the scene of the crime.

Frank has cooperated with police officers before.

Frank has been in police stations many times, but has never been charged with a crime.

Pointing at Frank decreased the victim's credibility.

Frank's organization fights crime.

CASE 24 SOLUTION

Frank is a police officer who was added to the line-up.

THE CASE

150 people sit patiently in a train station waiting for their train. Suddenly, a voice announces the train has been canceled and 147 of the people get up and leave the station. Three people remain behind.

THE MYSTERY

Why didn't the three people leave the train station and where is the station located?

THE CLUES

The three people heard the announcement.

The three people are American.

The station is in Europe.

The station is in a country that had a famous wall torn down in 1989.

The three people speak only one language.

CASE 25 SOLUTION

The train station is in Germany and the three people don't speak German.

More 30 SECOND
MYSTERIES
WHY

Case 26

THE CASE

A person is fluent in many tongues and can easily communicate with everyone encountered while traveling. Most of the time the person speaks, however, no one can understand a word that is said.

THE MYSTERY

Why don't people understand most of the languages and what is the person's profession?

THE CLUES

The person is a man.

The man is a native English speaker.

Most of those who he talks to cannot speak English.

The man communicates with beings that are not human.

The man is a famous fictional doctor.

CASE 26 SOLUTION

The man is a doctor (Dr. Doolittle) who has the unusual ability to speak with animals.

Case 27

THE CASE

A man with a British accent travels from city to city in 2003, meeting and greeting people several times a week. He asks for help, as he has since the 1960s, but he doesn't really expect any, nor does he actually need any. Each night people respond to his pleas for help by cheering and clapping.

THE MYSTERY

Why is the man asking for "Help"?

THE CLUES

Since the 1960s, he has visited cities all around the world.

For a while there was a rumor that he was dead.

His first official visit to the USA was on February 11, 1964.

He used to get by with a little help from three famous friends.

He was a member of what's considered one of the greatest songwriting teams ever.

CASE 27 SOLUTION

The man, Paul McCartney, is performing his song "Help!" while on tour.

More 30 SECOND
MYSTERIES

WHY

Case 28

THE CASE

Martha works in a dark room at a round table. She isn't a manicurist or a sculptor, but hands are very important to her. She met Michael, talked with him briefly and took money from him.

THE MYSTERY

Why does Martha take Michael's money?

THE CLUES

Holding a person's hand is a very important aspect of Martha's job.

Her job requires a very special gift.

Michael wanted her opinion.

Sometimes Martha has to give someone bad news. She hates this part of her job.

Not everyone believes in Martha's gift.

CASE 28 SOLUTION

Martha is a palm reader. She took Michael's money because he was paying her for a reading.

ABOUT THE AUTHOR

Always ahead of the game, Bob Moog's newest undertaking is truly novel. As a game inventor, his credits include such favorites as *20 Questions*® and *30 Second Mysteries*®. As the CEO of University Games, he has propelled the company he founded with his college pal into an international operation that now boasts five divisions and over 350 products. Whether hosting his radio show "Games People Play," advising MBA candidates or inventing games, Bob sees work as serious fun. He now brings his flair for fun and learning to the bookshelf with the Spinner Books line.

Jeff Pinsker's involvement with mysteries began at an early age, with his avid readership of Encyclopedia Brown books (although he wasn't very good at solving the mysteries--maybe that's why he turned to writing them later in life). He graduated from Stanford University with three degrees, although how he accomplished this was a mystery to most of his classmates. He then ran a company that performed practical jokes for pay before joining University Games, where he invented and produced hundreds of board games. Not satisfied with games as the sole outlet for the arcane bits of knowledge stored away in his brain, he turned to creating 30 second mysteries and his other passion, crossword puzzles (if you enjoy the twisted mysteries in this book, be sure to check out his other University Games titles: *Comic Crosswords* and *Armchair Puzzlers: Crosswords*). Between writing projects, Jeff and a partner founded Infinitoy®, a small, but happy, toy company that makes ZOOB® construction toys and the QUIZMO® handheld electronic question and answer game.

Enjoy Spinner Books?
Get an original game!

Find these games and more at AreYouGame.com
or your nearest toy store.

2030 Harrison Street, San Francisco, CA 94110
1-800-347-4818, www.ugames.com